# SMART Board™ Lessons: Expository Writing

40 Ready-to-Use, Motivating Lessons on CD to Help You Teach Essential Writing Skills



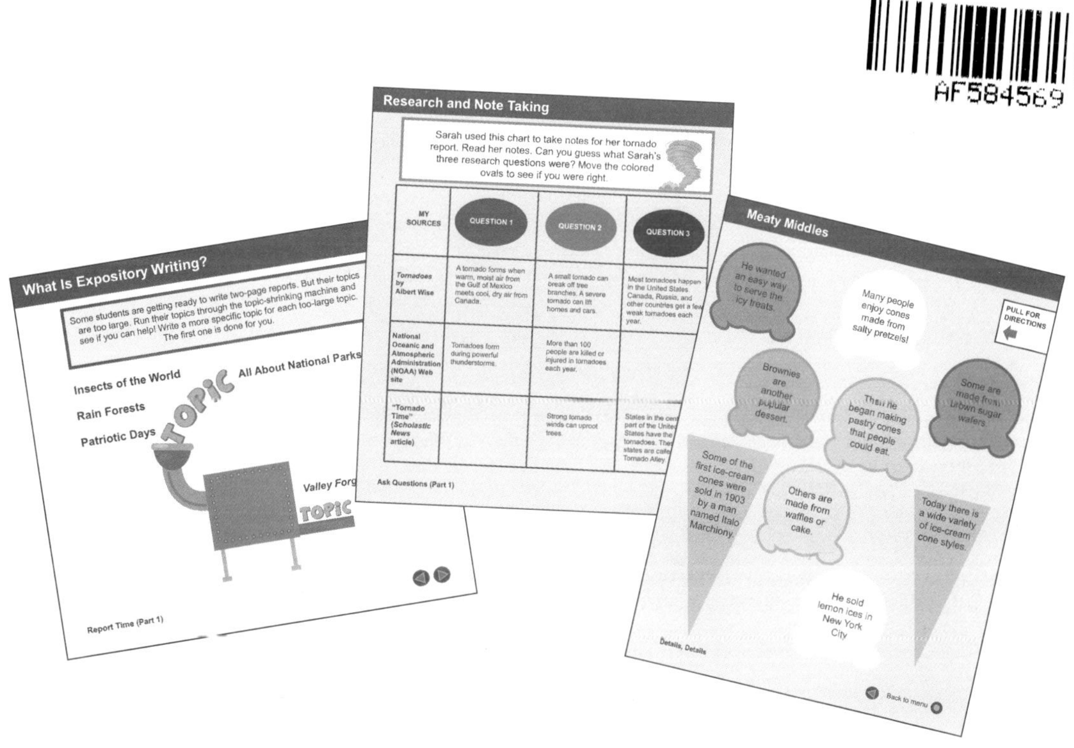


By Karen Kellaher

New York • Toronto • London • Auckland • Sydney
Mexico City • New Delhi • Hong Kong • Buenos Aires

Teaching Resources

*For Jack, who loves facts*





Edited by Maria L. Chang and Betsy Henry Pringle

Illustrations by Kelly J. Brownlee

Cover design by Brian LaRossa

Designed by Rosanna Brockley

Design assistance by Aileen Morrow

Art direction by Sarah Baynes

Production by Jennifer Marx

*SMART Board™ Lessons: Expository Writing*
is produced by **becker&mayer!**, Bellevue, WA 98004

ISBN-13: 978-0-545-28511-7

ISBN-10: 0-545-28511-9

10835



Printed, manufactured, and assembled in Hong Kong, China

1 2 3 4 5 6 7 8 9 10 16 15 14 13 12 11

# Contents

# Introduction

Looking for a way to energize your writing curriculum? The perfect tool is hanging on your classroom wall! By using your SMART Board™ to teach writing genres and skills, you can bring the writing process to life and model how to form ideas, choose words, organize information, and much more. You will discover many advantages over more traditional methods:

- The SMART Board offers instant lesson engagement. Whether you are teaching about nouns, narratives, or Roman numerals, you will have students' immediate attention. Many of today's kids were computer literate even before they started school. They are accustomed to games and gadgets that respond to the touch of a fingertip. A SMART Board grabs their attention in a way that blackboards and handouts fail to do.
- Because it offers a large, interactive display and opportunities for collaborative learning, the SMART Board is a smart way to teach students 21st-century skills like working in teams, marking text electronically, synthesizing information, organizing data, interpreting visual aids, and evaluating Web sites. These skills are an increasingly important part of the standards in many states.
- The SMART Board is easy to use, even for technophobes. Using the board itself and the accompanying Notebook software is fairly intuitive. On the interactive whiteboard, you can do anything you can do on your computer screen—and then some. So even if you are just starting out, you can pull off a fun, effective lesson. The lessons on the attached CD will make it easy.

## About the CD and Book

Make the most of SMART technology within your language arts curriculum. The SMART Notebook pages on the CD are a perfect way to teach writing skills because they allow you to model concepts and skills for the whole class. You can read and analyze examples of expository writing together, deciding what kinds of leads grab a reader's attention and what order of information makes the most sense. You can move, highlight, underline, and change text right on the whiteboard. And best of all, you can save everything for later use or review. Distribute copies of the completed Notebook pages for students to have on hand as rule reminders.

The CD contains five units on expository writing. Each unit is on the CD as a Notebook file with several interactive pages. These pages take advantage of the bells and whistles SMART technology has to offer without being overwhelming to the SMART Board novice. You'll find opportunities to use the Creative Pens, on-screen keyboard, graphic organizers, cloning tools, drag-and-drop feature, and much more. Instructions for using each SMART tool are embedded in the lesson plans.

Each unit on the CD introduces writing skills in a gradual-release format. The first lesson in each unit introduces the topic, engages students' attention, and establishes what they already know. In the next few lessons, students collaboratively explore concrete skills related to the topic. In the last "lesson," students synthesize and apply what they have learned in a brief independent assignment. You may choose to have students complete this final Your Turn! activity in class or as a homework assignment.

This book contains easy-to-use lessons corresponding to each CD unit. Lessons include objectives, pacing suggestions, and step-by-step directions for teaching with each SMART Notebook file on the CD. They also correlate with important language arts standards.

## Tech Tips

Although the SMART Expository Writing CD was created using Notebook 10 software, you will be able to use the activities with older versions of the software. If you are still getting the hang of your SMART Board, be sure to look for the technology tips offered at various points throughout the units. However, the following is an overview of the main Notebook features you will be using.

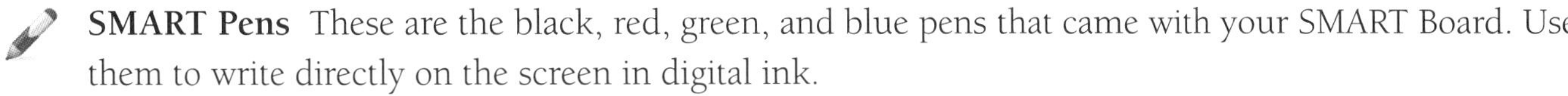

**SMART Pens** These are the black, red, green, and blue pens that came with your SMART Board. Use them to write directly on the screen in digital ink.

**Creative Pens** A student favorite, this tool allows you to draw fun lines made of smiley faces, stars, rainbow stripes, and more.

**Magic Pen** When students circle text or art with the Magic Pen, a spotlight focuses on the circled portion of the page. Everything else on the page goes dark temporarily. It's a dramatic way to focus attention on one element on a page!

**Eraser** Like its old-fashioned counterpart, this eraser removes unwanted writing. It will work on text and lines created with the SMART pens. It will not work on typed text or art objects.

**On-Screen Keyboard** If your students are adding text to a small field or simply prefer typing to writing freehand, use the on-screen keyboard. You can access it by touching the keyboard icon on the front tray of your SMART Board.

**Properties Tool** In several of the activities in this book, you will be guided to use this feature to change the color or style of a SMART pen or to add color to a box.

**Screen Shade** A teacher favorite, this tool allows you to cover part of a page while focusing attention on another part. Activate the shade by clicking on the Screen Shade icon on your toolbar. Deactivate it by clicking again. To gradually open a shade that covers your screen, use one of the circular buttons on the shade itself to drag the shade open.

UNIT 1

# What Is Expository Writing?

**Use these interactive Notebook pages to introduce the purpose and characteristics of expository writing and to explore the many forms expository writing can take.**

## OBJECTIVES

Students will be able to:

✓ Understand the purpose and common elements of expository writing.

✓ Analyze examples of expository writing.

✓ Recognize that there are many distinct forms of expository writing, including research reports, compare/contrast essays, how-to essays, cause/effect essays, news articles, and biographies.

## TIME

About 3–4 class periods for Unit 1 (allow 15–20 minutes per lesson)

## MEETING THE STANDARDS

This lesson correlates to the following writing standards for grades 3 through 6:

- Understand how writing can be adapted for different audiences and purposes.
- Recognize that expository text is writing that is intended to explain or inform.

## GETTING READY

Before students arrive, have your SMART Board ready to go. Load the SMART Expository Writing CD onto your host computer and copy the **1 What Is Expository Writing?** Notebook file onto your hard drive. Open the local file. The first interactive page, the *What Is Expository Writing?* menu, will appear on your SMART Board. To display the Notebook pages for each of the eight lessons in this unit, click on the button next to the name of the lesson.

## INTRODUCING THE CONCEPT

### What Is Expository Writing?

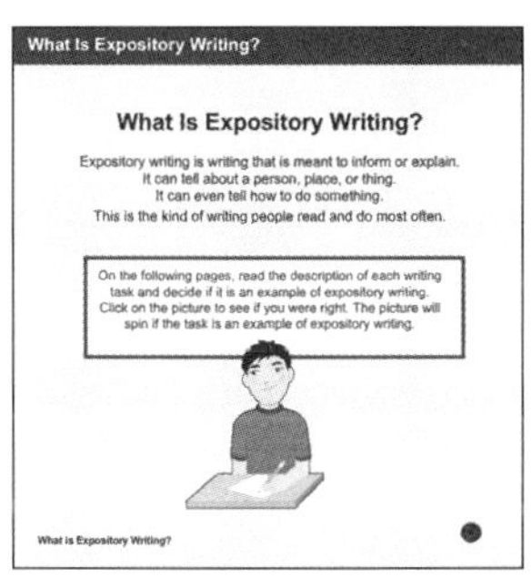


1. Display *What Is Expository Writing?* on the SMART Board. To begin, read the purpose of *expository writing* given in the introduction (to inform or explain). Elicit examples from the class of pieces of expository writing they have read recently, either at home or at school. Some common examples include textbooks, nonfiction trade books, Web sites, newspapers or magazines, instruction manuals, even notes from Mom on how to start the dishwasher. Remind students that expository writing is different from *narrative writing* (usually meant to entertain) and *persuasive writing* (meant to persuade or convince).
2. Read the directions together and click on the right arrow to go to the next page. Have a student read aloud the first sample writing task. Together, discuss Jorge's reason for writing. Ask: *Is he writing to persuade, to entertain, or to inform?* Remind students that if Jorge's purpose is to explain or inform, his writing is expository. Have students click on the skateboard illustration to check their understanding. Point out that the image will spin if the example is indeed expository.
3. Repeat step 2 with the remaining sample writing tasks on the page. For each one, check students' response by having a volunteer touch the accompanying image to see if it spins. The examples of expository writing in this activity are:

- Jorge's steps for skateboarding
- Mr. Dietrich's article for the paper
- Jessica's cat report
- May's paragraph about her brother

4. Review with students why the other two writing tasks are not expository. *(Olivia's haunted house story is narrative, meant to entertain. Daniel's letter is persuasive.)*
5. Point out that in the next several lessons, students will explore some of the interesting forms expository writing can take.

**TECH TIP**

Remember that on a SMART Board, a tap of your finger is like a click of the mouse on your desktop computer. To activate an animated shape like those on this page, just tap the screen with a finger. If the expected animation does not work, try again, tapping more firmly.

## INTERACTIVE LEARNING

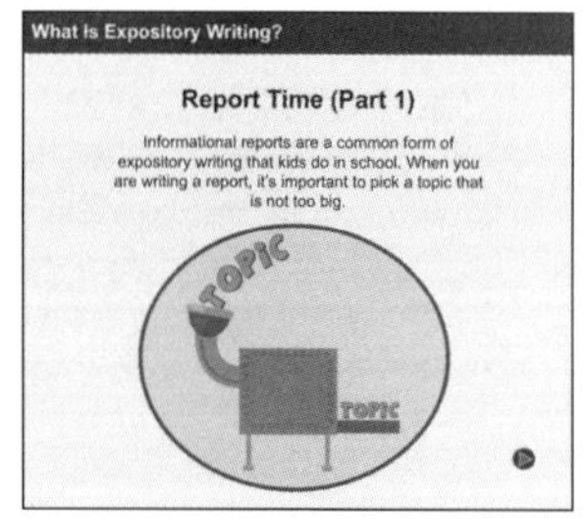


### Report Time (Parts 1 and 2)

1. Ask students if they have ever written reports for school. Elicit a few examples of topics they have covered. Explain that research reports are one of the most common kinds of expository writing kids will do during their school years. In elementary school, reports may be only a page or two, but by the time they are in high school, students will be writing much longer reports.
2. Display *Report Time (Part 1)* on the SMART Board and read the introduction. Guide students to understand that picking a good topic is a key part of writing a good report. Point out that one common mistake students make is to choose topics that are too large. When a topic is too large and general, the resulting report sounds vague and incomplete. A two-page report on sports, for example, would hardly even begin to cover the basics. A smaller topic allows the writer to cover the topic completely and with specific details. For example, a two-page report on lacrosse could have a paragraph each on the equipment, rules, and origins of the game. This topic is much more manageable than the broad topic of "sports."
3. Click on the right arrow to go to the next page. Read the directions together. Show that the topic-shrinking machine made the sample topic "All About National Parks" more manageable by downsizing it to "Valley Forge National Park." Now the writer can focus on one park's specific features and history. Drag the topics to one side.
4. Read aloud the first topic on the page, "Insects of the World," and move it next to the "input" side (top) of the topic-shrinking machine. Have students discuss some ways they could downsize the topic into something more specific. Examples include: mosquitoes, houseflies, wasps, and Japanese beetles. Choose a favorite specific report topic and use one of the SMART pens to jot it down on the "output" side of the machine.
5. Repeat step 4 with the remaining two topics. Some ideas include:

- **Rain Forests:** The Amazon Rain Forest, Medicines from the Rain Forest, Rain Forest Frogs
- **Patriotic Days:** Independence Day, Veterans Day, Memorial Day

6. Now, display *Report Time (Part 2)* on the SMART Board and read the introduction. Explain that while some topics are too big, others can be too small. A too-tight topic can make it hard to find enough information for a report.
7. Drag the directions onto the page and read them aloud. Work together to identify topics that may be too small, and have students circle them with the Magic Pen.

**TECH TIP**

Don't forget to put your tools away when you are finished with them! After you use a tool like the Magic Pen, be sure to go back to the selector tool (plain black arrow) before continuing with other tasks.

8. Discuss ways to broaden each topic enough to make an interesting and fact-filled report. Emphasize that the size of the topic may vary somewhat with the length of a report. Some suggestions include:

| | | |
|---|---|---|
| Where Amelia Earhart Grew Up | → | Amelia Earhart |
| Winds During a Hurricane | → | How Hurricanes Are Measured |
| What Plant Stems Do | → | The Parts of a Plant |

## A "How-To"

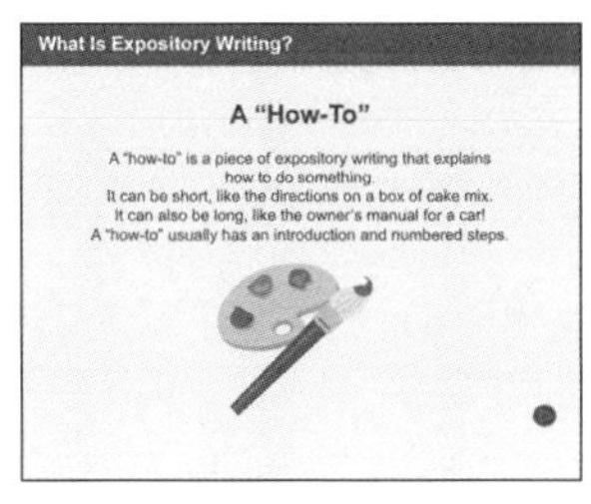


1. Ask students how many of them have followed written directions to make or build something. Discuss their experiences and ask if the directions were easy or difficult to follow. Use students' comments to highlight some characteristics of "good" directions. For example:

   - The directions tell you exactly what to do and do not leave anything to your imagination.
   - The directions are numbered so that you know the order in which you should do things.

2. Point out that like reports, directions on how to make or do something are an example of expository writing. These directions are sometimes described as "how-to" essays. Display *A "How-To"* on the SMART Board and read the introduction together.
3. Click on the right arrow and read the directions. Have students get out a piece of scrap paper and write detailed directions for how to draw an everyday object. It can be any shape or image students please, as long as they can express how to create the image without using the name of the object. Emphasize that students should keep their subjects and directions private until further notice.
4. When students have finished, click on the right arrow to go to the next page. Call on a student volunteer to slowly read his or her directions. Use a SMART pen to draw the image inside the box, following the student's directions, one step at a time. Even if you begin to recognize the object you are drawing, be sure to stick to the oral directions. When you finish, see if you and the class can identify the intended object from your drawing. (Note: You may choose to have a student volunteer draw at the board instead of doing this step yourself.)
5. Discuss challenges you encountered as you completed the exercise. For example, you might say: *When Steven told me to draw a circle inside the rectangle, I wasn't sure where to put it. How could this instruction have been more specific?*
6. If you'd like, repeat the drawing exercise using another student's directions.

### TECH TIP

If your "how-to" instructions call for drawing basic shapes like triangles, circles, or rectangles, SMART Notebook has two tools that can help you perfect your artistry! Go to the Shapes tool to select a predrawn basic shape. Or, use the Shape Recognition pen to draw a shape on your own. The software should recognize the shape you are trying to draw and snap the lines into place.

## News Flash

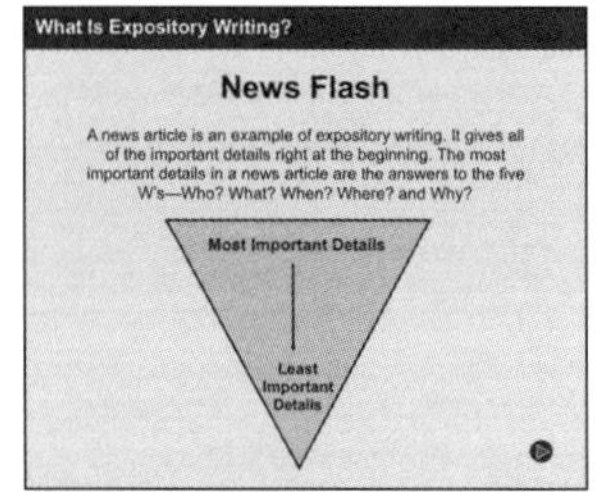


1. Display *News Flash* on the SMART Board and read the introduction aloud. Review with students how they know that a news article is an example of expository writing. *(It is meant to inform or explain.)*
2. Point out that the yellow inverted triangle on this page demonstrates the unique nature of a news article: *All of the most important facts appear near the beginning of the article*. Explain that there is a historical reason for this writing style. Long before there were desktop computers and word processing software, editors would check pages in a composing room, where the articles were pasted onto page layouts. Articles that were too long had to be trimmed down quickly. The fastest way was to simply chop off the overflow using a sharp blade. As long as the important facts were all at the beginning, the editor knew that he or she was not cutting anything crucial to the article.
3. Review that in a news article, the important facts answer the five *W*s: *who, what, when, where,* and *why*. (You might explain that *how* is another important question that is often addressed.)
4. Click on the right arrow to go to the next page and read the directions on the pull tab. Have students read the news article aloud. Pull out the color key and use it to underline these five *W*s.

| | |
|---|---|
| **Who?** | Jack Packard, a 4-year-old |
| **What?** | Drove a car |
| **When?** | Tuesday at 10:00 a.m. |
| **Where?** | Downtown Smithfield |
| **Why?** | To feed Snowball, his school's guinea pig |

5. To underline neatly in different colors, use the Lines tool on your toolbar. First, select the regular straight line with no arrows. Then, click on the Properties menu on the left side of your screen and go to Line Style. Choose a color from the palette that appears and use your line tool to underline the desired piece of text. Go back to Properties > Line Style to change the line color for the next piece of text you want to underline.

## That's Life!

1. In this activity, students will recognize biographies and autobiographies as examples of expository writing. Display *That's Life!* on the SMART Board and read the introduction together. Ask students if they have ever read a person's life story, and discuss some examples. Review the directions and then click on the right arrow to go to the next page.

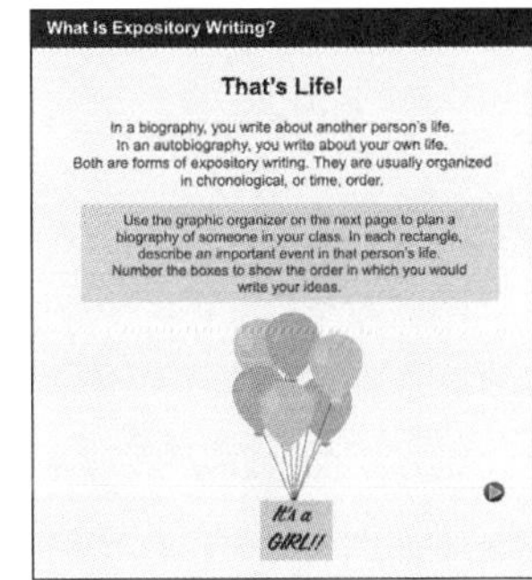


2. To prepare for the activity, have students list important events from their lives on scrap paper. Then ask for one volunteer to share his or her lifetime events with the class.
3. Use one of the SMART pens to record the volunteer's name in the center of the organizer and some events from the student's life in the outside rectangles. Examples of important events might include:

- Birth
- Births of siblings
- A move to a new home
- Start of school
- Start of a favorite activity (soccer, dance, etc.)
- Getting a pet
- Learning a skill (riding a bike, etc.)

4. Review that writers usually organize biographies and autobiographies in chronological order because that is the order in which the events happened. Explain that life stories do not usually include trivial or minor details. Instead, the writer focuses on important events that helped shape the person they are writing about.
5. If you wish, repeat the activity with one or two additional volunteers.

## Cause and Effect

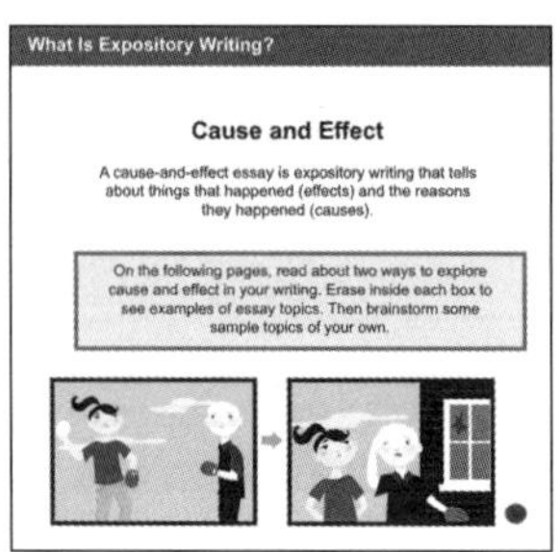


1. Display *Cause and Effect* on the SMART Board and read the introduction. Guide students to understand that a cause-and-effect essay explores the reasons an event happened or the effects that happened because of an event. Share some examples of cause-and-effect questions:

   - What led to the Revolutionary War?
   - What are the causes of global warming?
   - What are the effects of earthquakes?

2. Read the directions together and then click on the right arrow. Have a student read aloud the text above the purple graphic organizer, then have him or her erase the purple box to reveal some examples.
3. As a class, brainstorm other examples of essay topics that describe the causes of an event. Using the SMART pens, add these ideas to the bottom portion of the purple organizer.
4. Click on the right arrow and repeat steps 2 and 3 for the green graphic organizer. In this organizer, students will brainstorm examples of topics that tell about the effects of a chosen event.
5. Explain that sometimes, students may need to write a whole essay that explores causes and effects. But they may also find that they explore causes and effects in other forms of expository writing, such as research reports, biographies, and news articles.

### TECH TIP

**If students have trouble writing with the SMART pen, check that they are holding the stylus correctly. If a student's wrist or hand rubs against the board while he or she is writing, the words on the board may appear garbled and illegible. When using a SMART pen, only the stylus tip should make contact with the SMART Board.**

## Compare and Contrast (Parts 1 and 2)

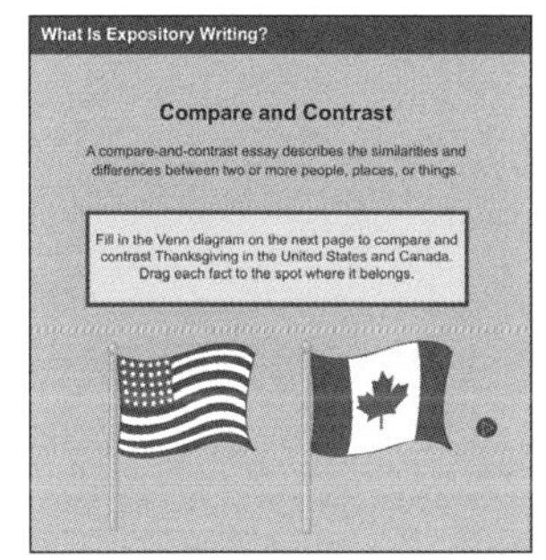


1. Display *Compare and Contrast* on the SMART Board and explain that a compare-and-contrast essay is the last form of expository writing that students will explore in this unit. Read the introductory material together and ask students to complete the following prompts:

   - When we compare two or more things, we look for ______.
     *(ways they are the same)*
   - When we contrast two or more things, we look for ______.
     *(ways they are different)*

2. Read the directions aloud and then click on the right arrow to reveal the Venn diagram. If necessary, review the structure of a Venn diagram: *The circle on the left is for facts that describe one topic. The circle on the right is for facts that describe the second topic. The overlapping area in the center is for facts that describe both.*
3. Read aloud the descriptions of the Canadian and American Thanksgivings.
4. Demonstrate how to drag a piece of text with a finger. Then ask a volunteer to read the first descriptive phrase under "Canadian Thanksgiving." Have him or her drag the text to the appropriate spot on the diagram.
5. Repeat step 4 with the remaining descriptive phrases. Phrases that describe both holidays should appear only in the center of the diagram.
6. When you finish the diagram, click on the right arrow to display *Compare and Contrast (Part 2)*. Guide students to understand that when you want to compare and contrast two items, there are several ways to organize your writing. Two of those ways are explored on this page and the next. Pull out the directions onto the page and read them together.
7. Read aloud the first way to organize a compare-and-contrast essay. Then have a student drag the purple box to one side. An essay that follows this organizational format will appear. Go over it with students; if you wish, use the SMART pens to write numbers on the text to show where the text corresponds to the organizational plan. Put the box back into place.
8. Click on the right arrow to go to the next page. Repeat step 7 for the yellow box. Discuss which method for comparing and contrasting students prefer.

### TECH TIP

If students have trouble dragging and dropping the pieces of text, demonstrate the process yourself. Explain that students should not take their finger off the SMART Board once they have touched the text or image they wish to move. The drag function works best when the user's finger stays in contact with the board.

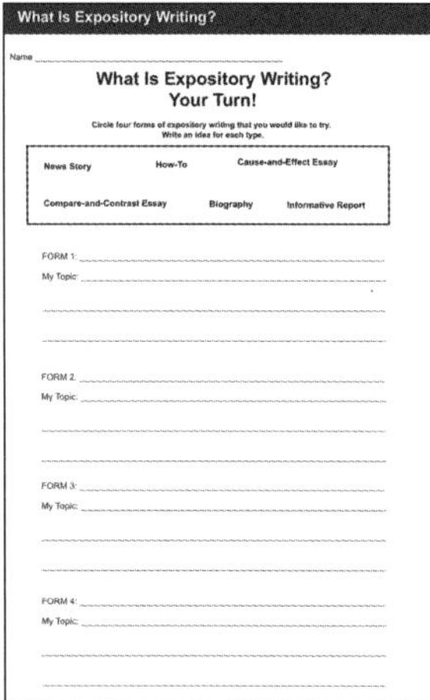
What Is Expository Writing?

Name

What Is Expository Writing?
Your Turn!

Circle four forms of expository writing that you would like to try.
Write an idea for each type.

News Story | How-To | Cause-and-Effect Essay
Compare-and-Contrast Essay | Biography | Informative Report

FORM 1:
My Topic:

FORM 2:
My Topic:

FORM 3:
My Topic:

FORM 4:
My Topic:

## What Is Expository Writing? Your Turn!

1. Print and make copies of *What Is Expository Writing? Your Turn!* Display the Notebook page on the SMART Board and distribute copies of the worksheet. Explain that students will complete this page on their own to apply what they have learned about expository writing so far.
2. Review the directions with students, explaining that they will come up with topics for four distinct forms of expository writing. Emphasize that they may choose any four forms listed on the page. Remind them to:

- Keep research report topics "just right" in size.
- Choose topics that really interest them.
- Use real-life news events for news article topics.
- Name two people, places, or things for a compare-and-contrast topic.

3. Have students complete the exercise in class or as a homework assignment. As you move forward with the lessons on the CD, you may want to have students use their topics to research and write an actual piece of expository text.

# Research and Note Taking

## UNIT 2

**This series of interactive Notebook pages tackles all the skills students will need to get started in expository writing, from formulating research questions to crediting sources.**

### OBJECTIVES

Students will be able to:

- ✓ Form questions to guide research.
- ✓ Use keywords to research topics on the Web.
- ✓ Use tables of contents and indexes to research topics in books.
- ✓ Evaluate the credibility of an Internet source.
- ✓ Correctly credit sources of information.

### TIME

About 3–4 class periods for Unit 2 (allow 15–20 minutes per lesson)

### MEETING THE STANDARDS

This lesson correlates to the following writing standards for grades 3 through 6:

- Apply a variety of prewriting strategies in order to generate and structure ideas.
- Conduct research on issues by generating ideas and questions.
- Use a variety of technological and information resources.

### GETTING READY

Before students arrive, have your SMART Board ready to go. Load the SMART Expository Writing CD onto your host computer and copy the **2 Research & Note Taking** Notebook file onto your hard drive. Open the local file. The first interactive page, the *Research and Note Taking* menu, will appear on your SMART Board. To display the Notebook pages for each of the eight lessons in this unit, click on the button next to the name of the lesson.

# INTRODUCING THE CONCEPT

## Research and Note Taking

1. Display *Research and Note Taking* on the SMART Board and read the introduction. Ask students to share what they already know about doing research. Then click on the right arrow to go to the next page. Pull out the directions and read them together. Explain that students will take this true-or-false quiz to see how much they know about doing research.
2. Have a student volunteer read the first true-or-false statement aloud. Ask the student to give his or her answer orally, then discuss the response with the class to see who agrees or disagrees. Have your student volunteer click on "true" or "false." If the response is correct, the shape will spin!
3. Have the volunteer erase inside the red box directly under the first question to reveal more information about this topic.
4. Repeat steps 2 and 3 with the remaining true-or-false statements. Discuss with students any answers they find surprising.

- Research begins with asking questions. TRUE
- Now that the Internet is available, books are not very useful. FALSE
- It's a good idea to use one trustworthy source for most of the facts in your report or essay. FALSE
- Using another writer's exact words is a form of stealing. TRUE
- Interviewing someone is a good way to get information. TRUE

**TECH TIP**

When using your SMART eraser for an activity like this one, remind students to rub the eraser over only the box being discussed. Erasing over other boxes will reveal the answers prematurely.

## INTERACTIVE LEARNING

### Ask Questions (Parts 1 and 2)

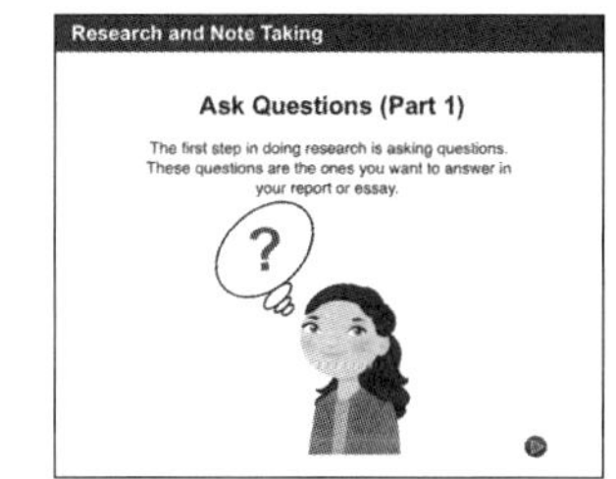


1. Display *Ask Questions (Part 1)* on the SMART Board. Read the introduction aloud and click on the right arrow to go to the next page. Point out that making a chart like the one shown is a good way to start the research process. Along the top row, the writer jots down questions that he or she would like to address in the report or essay. In the left-hand column, he or she lists sources. Inside the grid, the writer can record what each source has to say about each question. This structure makes it very easy for the writer to go back later and find all of the facts he or she has collected on a specific question. It also makes it easy for the writer to credit sources. (More on that later in this unit!)
2. Review the directions and the filled-in chart together. Have one student name the three sources the report writer has used so far. Discuss the type of source each entry represents (book, Web site, article, other).
3. Have a student read aloud the facts in the column under Question 1. Discuss what question or subtopic these facts all seem to relate to. *(How do tornadoes form?* or *What causes a tornado?)* Invite your volunteer to drag the oval away from the top of the column to reveal the question.
4. Repeat step 3 for the remaining two columns of facts. *(Question 2: What damage do tornadoes do? Question 3: Where do tornadoes happen?* Note that students may phrase these questions slightly differently.)
5. Point out that as the writer proceeds to draft his or her tornado report, he or she could create a paragraph or section for each of these guiding questions. The chart structure would make it easy to locate the facts that belong in each section.
6. Click on the right arrow to display *Ask Questions (Part 2)*. Read the directions on the pull-out tab. Explain that this page offers students a chance to practice generating research questions.
7. Allow student volunteers to use the SMART pens to write possible research questions in the boxes. Some examples are listed below. Explain that students will be brainstorming similar questions for their topics when they get ready to write their own reports or essays.

**Siberian Tigers**

- What is their habitat?
- What is their diet?
- What do they look like?

**The White House**

- What is inside?
- When was it built?
- Who has lived there?

**Puerto Rico**

- What is the climate like?
- Where is it located?
- What do the people like to do?

## Find Facts Fast

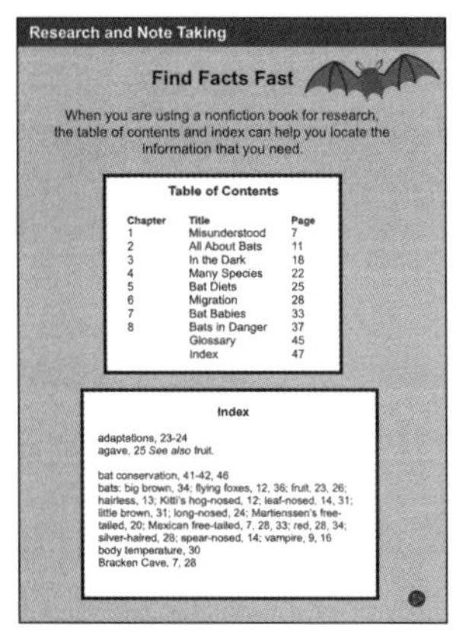


1. Display *Find Facts Fast* on the SMART Board and read the introduction together. Discuss briefly where you would find a book's table of contents *(in the front)* and index *(in the back)*. Ask students if they have ever used these tools to locate information in a book. If you have one handy, show students a real-life example of each. (Most textbooks contain both a table of contents and an index.)
2. Point out that a table of contents usually gives chapter numbers, chapter titles, and starting page numbers. An index lists all subtopics discussed in a book. It might give a page range (two page numbers separated by a dash) or individual page numbers (page numbers separated by commas) where that subtopic is discussed. A table of contents is like a general overview, while an index is specific and detailed.
3. Click on the right arrow to go to the next page and pull the tab to read the directions. Call on a student to tackle the first bat question. Have the student give the answer and name which tool (table of contents or index) helped him or her answer that type of question. Have the student drag aside the bat image at the end of the question to check his or her answer.
4. Repeat step 3 for the questions on the following three pages. Discuss students' thinking.

**Answers:**

**1. Chapter 5, Bat Diets:** I used the table of contents because it asked for the chapter.

**2. Pages 9 and 16:** I used the index because it named a specific kind of bat that did not appear in the table of contents and asked for specific page numbers.

**3. Fruit:** I used the index because *agave* is one of the index entries. The "see also" note in italics helped me understand that agave is a type of fruit.

**4. Why people think bats are scary:** I used the table of contents because the question asked for a general prediction about a chapter.

5. Have students generate additional questions for one another using the table of contents and the index.

## The Search Is On

1. Display *The Search Is On* on the SMART Board and read the introduction. Activate prior knowledge by asking students to describe where they go when they need to find information on the Internet. Students will likely name Google, Yahooligans, MSN Search, and other search engines. Explain that these are called *search engines*, and that like car engines, they are only as good as the "fuel" or information a searcher puts in. There are billions of pages on the Web. By entering the right instructions, a searcher can find the handful of pages that are just right for his or her needs.

2. Read the directions aloud and explain that a *search term* is a keyword or phrase that an Internet searcher wants to know more about. When the searcher enters a search term into a search engine, the search engine's software will look for sites that include that keyword or phrase.

3. Click on the right arrow and have students read the first search scenario. Taylor is writing about humpback whales, so she enters the keyword *whales* into the search engine. Have students discuss what Taylor's challenge is *(the search returned too many pages)* and how she could fix the problem *(she could add the descriptor* humpback *to her search term)*. Invite a student volunteer to use a SMART pen to write the new search terms in the box.

4. Click on the right arrow and repeat step 3 for the second search scenario. Jacob is writing a report called "How Soccer Got Its Start." He enters the title of his report into a search engine. Discuss Jacob's challenge *(none of the sites that show up have the information he is looking for)*. Together, brainstorm what Jacob could do differently. *(He could think of synonyms for the kind of information he is looking for and use them in his search. For example, he could enter* soccer history *or* soccer invention.*)* Invite a student volunteer to write the new search term in the box.

5. Use the activity to review basic tips for conducting Internet searches:

- Be specific.
- Include multiple words (for most search engines, you no longer need to use the word *and*).
- Try synonyms or related words if an attempted search term fails.
- Check your spelling before hitting *search*. While most engines will automatically correct spelling, software spell checkers are not perfect and will not find homophone errors.

6. If time allows, log on to the Internet via your SMART Board and conduct a few actual searches with students using a school-approved search engine.

For this or other activities that call for writing, consider having students type their responses onto the screen instead of using the SMART pens. Activate your on-screen keyboard by touching the keyboard button on your SMART Board tray or by choosing the keyboard icon in your toolbar.

## Evaluate a Web Site

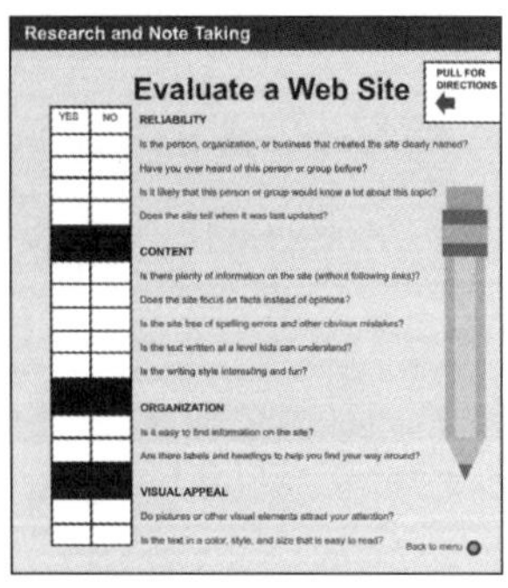


1. Engage students by asking: *Who's in charge of the Internet?* After some discussion, let students know that, in a way, this was a trick question. There is no one person or group that is in charge of monitoring Internet content. That means anyone can create a site on any topic they please. Throw out a few silly examples to demonstrate:
   - If I wanted to set up a site about rock climbing even though I had never climbed a rock in my life, could I do it? You bet!
   - If you wanted to create a site about *Escherichia coli,* could you do it? Absolutely—even if you had to look it up in a dictionary to find out what it is (a type of bacteria).
2. Point out that the open nature of the Internet puts a burden on researchers. Before trusting a site, researchers need to figure out who posted the information, when they did it, what their purpose was, and how accurate the information is. This type of evaluation lets the researcher stick to information posted by reputable and trustworthy organizations and people. Point out that sites run by the government end in the suffix *.gov*, while sites run by nonprofit organizations end in *.org*, and school-connected sites end in *.edu*.
3. Display *Evaluate a Web Site* on the SMART Board. Call on a student to use the SMART highlighter to mark the four criteria on which the class will be evaluating sites—reliability, content, organization, and visual appeal. Read the questions together, discussing why each one is important:

**Reliability:** These questions help students identify who created the site and when. This helps them weed out sites created by nonexperts and by groups with a special interest. (For example, a site created by a video-game maker about why video games are good for you.) This also helps students weed out sites that were created a long time ago and haven't been updated, especially critical in topics related to science and technology.

**Content:** These questions help students identify sites that are thorough, interesting, factual, and on level.

**Organization:** These questions help students focus their attention on sites that are easy to navigate and use.

**Visual Appeal:** These questions help students identify sites whose pictures, text style, and other graphics are pleasing to the eye.

4. Log on to your school Web site, another familiar site, or one of the suggested sites below. Together, use the checklist to evaluate the site on all four criteria.

http://www.worldwildlife.org

http://bensguide.gpo.gov/3-5/government/branches.html

http://kids.msfc.nasa.gov

## Interview Skills

1. Explain that sometimes, students may have specific questions about a topic that they cannot answer using traditional print or Web resources. In some of those cases, an interview with an expert may be in order.

2. Present the following situations, and challenge students to name the person (or type of person) they would interview for each one:

    - A report on what a mayor does *(the local mayor)*
    - A biography of a family member *(the family member)*
    - A news article on endangered ferrets *(an expert on ferrets)*

3. Display *Interview Skills* on the SMART Board and read the introduction together. Give an example of an open- and closed-ended question:
    - OPEN: What are some of the dangers ferrets face?
    - CLOSED: Do you work hard?
4. Click on the right arrow to go to the next page and read the directions on the pull-out tab. Explain that students will help Maggie choose four open-ended questions from the list of questions she has already brainstormed. Have a student volunteer read aloud the questions.
5. Call on a student to choose one open-ended question that Maggie could ask in order to get a lot of information from her subject. If the rest of the class agrees that it is a good, open-ended question, have the volunteer drag the question into one of the empty speech bubbles at the top of the page.
6. Repeat step 5 until each speech bubble has been filled with an open-ended question.
7. To wrap up, point out that professional interviewers do sometimes use closed-ended questions. However, they immediately follow up the question with an open-ended one. Some examples:
    - Do you enjoy your job? Why or why not?
    - Which country was your favorite vacation destination? Why?
8. As a culmination, have students work in pairs to practice asking one another open-ended questions.

## Give Credit

1. Ask students if they have ever heard the word *bibliography*. Explain that a bibliography is a list of books, Web sites, interviews, and other resources that a writer used to write a report. Explain that older students usually have to hand in a bibliography when they write a report. It's a good idea for younger students to get used to the practice, as well. Creating a bibliography gives credit to the original source of an idea and makes it easy to find more information at a later date.
2. Display *Give Credit* on the SMART Board and read the introduction. Then click on the right arrow and use the Screen Shade tool (or the Spotlight tool, if your version of Notebook has it) to focus students' attention on one entry at a time. For each entry, discuss what kind of resource it is (book, Web site, etc.) and what each part of the entry represents (author, publishing company, date published, city of publication, etc.)
3. Click on the right arrow and read aloud the directions in the pull-out tab. Demonstrate how students can move the entries around on the page to put them in alphabetical order. Invite a volunteer to find the item that would appear first and drag it to the top of the page. Repeat with the remaining entries until the entire list has been alphabetized.
4. If you or your school prefers a different bibliographic style, point out any differences at this time. Print this model bibliography and make copies for students' writing folders.

### TECH TIP

If you've never used the Spotlight tool before, you are in for a treat! Look for the Spotlight tool  in your toolbar. When you select this tool, a bright rectangle will illuminate the middle of your screen. The rest of your screen will go dark. Move the borders of the lighted rectangle to place the spotlight exactly where you want it. When you are ready to move on, simply go to the small downward arrow that appears in the lower right corner of the rectangle and select Exit.

# EXTENDED LEARNING

## Research and Note Taking: Your Turn!

Research and Note Taking

Name

**Research and Note Taking: Your Turn!**

Use the chart to list your research questions and take notes from three sources.

| MY SOURCES | QUESTION: | QUESTION: | QUESTION: |
|---|---|---|---|
| | | | |
| | | | |
| | | | |

1. Print and make copies of *Research and Note Taking: Your Turn!* Display the Notebook page on the SMART Board and distribute copies of the worksheet. Explain that students will complete this page on their own, either in class or for homework, to apply what they have learned about researching a piece of expository writing. If students are writing reports for class, have them use the topics they have selected. Otherwise, have them select topics for this exercise.
2. Review the directions with students, explaining that they will:

- List three questions they would like to answer in a report. (If they have more questions, they can use a second copy of the chart template.)
- Locate three sources of information on their topic and list these in the column on the left. (If you would like to specify particular types of sources, add this instruction verbally.)
- Take notes from each resource in the center of the chart.

3. Keep in mind that this assignment will take several days. Once students have completed their assignments, invite volunteers to share their work with the class.

UNIT 3

# Beginnings and Endings

**The beginning and ending of a report are the two parts readers remember most! In this series of Notebook pages, students learn to craft leads that draw readers in and endings that satisfy them.**

## OBJECTIVES

Students will be able to:

- ✓ Identify the characteristics of a strong expository beginning.
- ✓ Write expository leads that use questions, surprising facts, wordplay, and description.
- ✓ Write a clear thesis statement (or topic statement).
- ✓ Identify the characteristics of a strong expository ending and apply those characteristics to their own writing.

## TIME

About 3–4 class periods for Unit 3 (allow 15–20 minutes per lesson)

## MEETING THE STANDARDS

This lesson correlates with the following writing standard for grades 3 through 6:

- Write expository text with a clear introduction, body, and conclusion.
- Establish a central idea in relation to purpose and audience.

## GETTING READY

Before students arrive, have your SMART Board ready to go. Load the SMART Expository Writing CD onto your host computer and copy the **3 Beginnings and Endings** Notebook file onto your hard drive. Open the local file. The first interactive page, the *Beginnings and Endings* menu, will appear on your SMART Board. To display the Notebook pages for each of the eight lessons in this unit, click on the button next to the name of the lesson.

# INTRODUCING THE CONCEPT

## Beginnings and Endings (Parts 1 and 2)

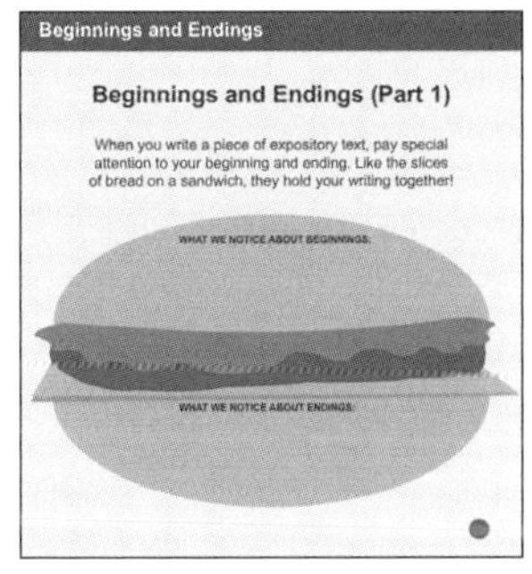


1. Display *Beginnings and Endings (Part 1)* on the SMART Board and read aloud the introduction. Discuss the slices of sandwich bread as a metaphor for the beginning and ending of a piece of expository text. Have students brainstorm what they think the job of the beginning (or *lead*) is. Repeat for the job of the expository ending.
2. Tell students they will return to the sandwich organizer in a moment, then click on the right arrow to display *Beginnings and Endings (Part 2)*. Read the directions on the pull-out tab. Have a student volunteer read the essay aloud. Then ask a second volunteer to read aloud just the beginning paragraph. Discuss what the writer is trying to do in this paragraph. You might ask: *What would the essay sound like without this opening paragraph?*
3. Display Parts 1 and 2 on the SMART Board at the same time, using the Dual/Single Page Display tool. As students make observations about the beginning, record their ideas in the sandwich organizer. For example, students may notice that:

    - A good beginning grabs readers' attention.
    - A good beginning makes you think, perhaps by asking a question.
    - A good beginning helps you connect the topic to yourself. (How do I get a snack when I am hungry?)
    - A good beginning gives the main idea for the whole report. It tells what the report will be about.

4. Once the top portion of the organizer is filled, explore the role of a good ending. On Part 2, have a student read aloud the last paragraph of the owl report. Discuss what the ending does for the report, and record students' ideas in the organizer on Part 1. Observations may include:

    - A strong ending repeats the main idea of the piece using different words.
    - A strong ending circles back to words or images that were brought up at the beginning (in this case, the ideas of fast prey and finding a meal).
    - A strong ending makes readers feel satisfied, like all important questions have been answered.

5. Print out and make copies of the graphic organizer for students' writing folders to help students remember and apply the characteristics of strong beginnings and endings.

### TECH TIP

To access the Dual/Single Page Display tool, go to the toolbar on your SMART Board display and click on the icon that resembles a computer monitor with two pages on it. Now, the two pages should appear on your board side by side.

## INTERACTIVE LEARNING

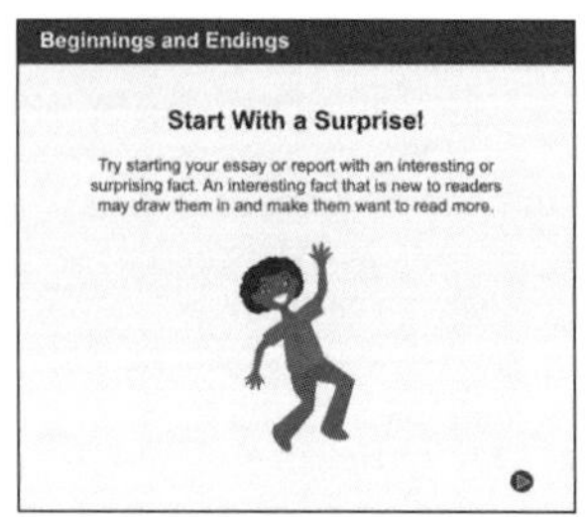


### Start With a Surprise!

1. Display *Start With a Surprise!* on the SMART Board and explain that this lesson explores one fun way to begin an expository report. An interesting fact that is new to readers may draw them in and make them want to read more.
2. Click on the right arrow and read the directions on the pull-out tab. Tell students that the writer wants to begin a report on cheetahs with a surprising fact. It is up to your students to choose the fact that they think will work best. Invite student volunteers to read aloud each cheetah fact.
3. Read the first fact *(They live in the open plains of Africa)* and ask students to raise their hands if they think the writer should begin with this fact. Emphasize that students can vote only once.
4. Allow each student who voted for the first fact to approach the SMART Board and use the Creative Pen to place a star on the line after the fact.
5. Repeat steps 3 and 4 for the remaining cheetah facts. When you finish, you should have a pictograph with one star representing each student vote. Have students count the stars after each fact and declare a winner.
6. Explain that hidden behind the cheetah pictures at the bottom of the screen are two examples of ways to use a fact as a lead. Both leads use the same fact, but in different ways. Invite a student volunteer to drag aside the first picture and read aloud the lead. Repeat for the second picture. Discuss which example students prefer, and why.
7. Remind students that they might want to try a "fun fact" lead on their next report or essay.

**TECH TIP**

Did you somehow end up with extra stars all over the page? Get rid of unwanted stars (or other shapes) by clicking back on the plain black arrow. Touch the shape you want to delete and then touch the red X (Delete tool) in your Notebook toolbar. You can also hit the back arrow (Undo tool) as many times as is necessary to clear the unwanted shapes.

## Start With a Question

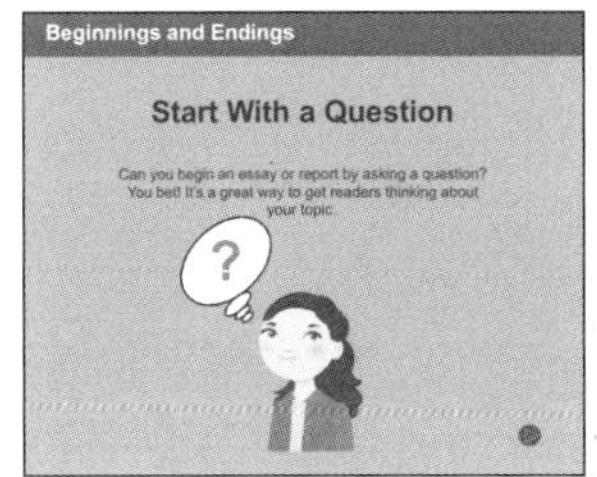


1. Display *Start With a Question* on the SMART Board and point out to students that this page does, indeed, start with a question! Explain that asking a question to make readers think is a great way to draw readers into a topic. It is a common and effective way to start a report or essay. In this lesson, students will explore some examples.
2. Click on the right arrow and pull on the tab to read the directions. Remind students that *lead* is another word for beginning. Have a student volunteer choose one of the question leads on the left side of the page and read it aloud. As a class, predict what that report would be about.
3. Have your volunteer drag the question he or she selected over to the crystal ball. As the question slides over the crystal ball, the next sentence or two of the report will be revealed. Have the student read the text inside the crystal ball aloud. Ask: *Were we correct in our prediction about the report's topic?*
4. Repeat step 3 for the remaining question leads. Discuss the different kinds of questions the writers used. Some, like the platypus question, are riddle-like. Others, like the spider question, are meant to set up a contrast between what the average reader thinks and what is actually true—a good technique to use when there are common misconceptions about a topic. Still others, like the paleontologist and White House leads, are designed to make readers imagine themselves in a situation.
5. Click the right arrow to go to the next page and read the Try It! prompt. Have students brainstorm questions they could use to begin an essay about their hometown. Have them imagine they are writing a travel brochure for the local chamber of commerce. Examples might include:

    - Where can you find both sandy beaches and rugged mountains?
    - What is there to do in New City?
    - Do you enjoy shopping and dining out?

6. Remind students that they might want to try a question lead on their next report or essay.

## Start With Wordplay

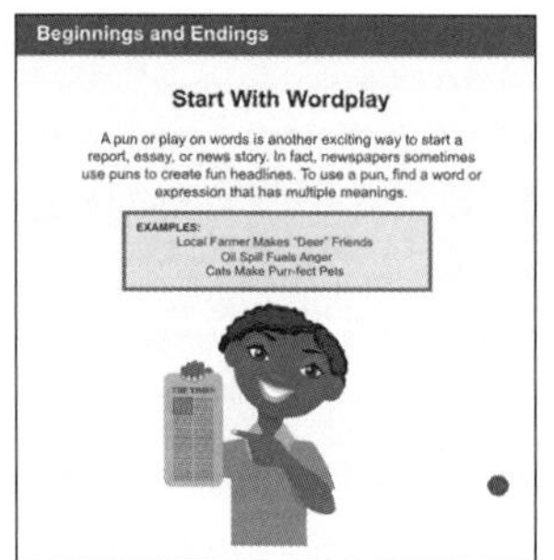


1. Display *Start With Wordplay* on the SMART Board. Read the introduction together and take a minute to talk about some examples of wordplay.

> **Some puns use words that sound the same but have different spellings and meanings.**
>
> EXAMPLE: Local Farmer Makes "Deer" Friends
>
> (This article is about how a farmer befriended deer that wandered onto his property.)

> **Other puns use words that look and sound the same but have different meanings. (Both meanings have to make sense with the topic.)**
>
> EXAMPLE: Veterinarians have found a new way to "treat" frightened patients.
>
> (This article talks about a way to give pets medicine in doggy treats. So "treat" is used in two ways.)

> **You can also play with words by rhyming or using alliteration (repetition of a beginning sound).**
>
> EXAMPLE: Move over, Rover. Experts say that by 2023, cats will replace dogs as America's top pet.

2. Click on the right arrow and review the directions together. Then read aloud the example of wordplay in the gorilla news story. Discuss the literal meaning of *ape* (a gorilla or other primate) and the figurative meaning of "going ape" (getting very excited).
3. Click on the right arrow and read aloud the text inside the thought bubble. To help students generate plays on words related to bees, first brainstorm a list of words we think of when we think of bees. You can record the words in SMART pen right on the screen. Your list might include words such as *hive, buzz, swarm, sting, fly,* and *honey.*
4. Ask students to look at the words and evaluate whether any of them have multiple meanings that would make effective beginnings. Point out that *buzz,* for example, is often used to mean "news." *Swarm* can refer to what bees do or what people do when they are in a large group.
5. Move the yellow thought bubble aside to reveal some examples of wordplay leads that might work for this topic.

6. Remind students to be on the lookout for opportunities to try a wordplay lead on reports and essays. However, point out that this kind of lead can take a long time to master.

## Start With a Scene

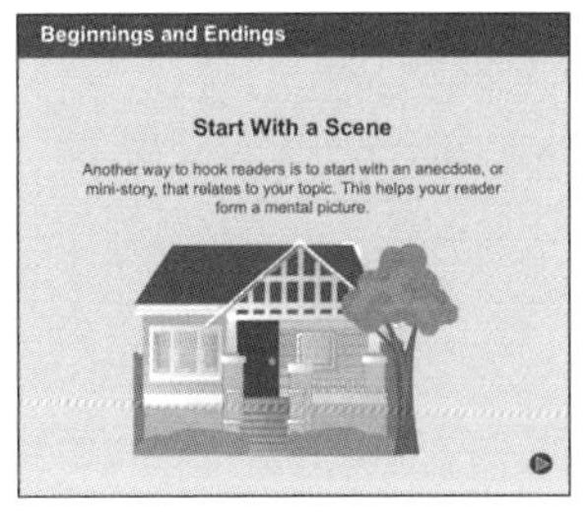


1. Remind students that they have already explored questions, surprising facts, and puns as ways to start expository text. Let them know that the last lead style they will explore in this unit is an *anecdote*, or very short story, that helps readers imagine the topic.
2. Display *Start With a Scene* on the SMART Board and read the introduction. Click on the right arrow and read the directions on the pull-out tab. Help students access the SMART highlighter from the toolbar for the activity. Use a finger to touch the Pen tool and select one of the highlighter colors from the pen menu (highlighter styles are on the far right). Remind students that a finger will now serve as the highlighter.
3. Have a student read aloud the sample anecdote about Mount Rushmore. Explain that students should look for words and phrases that help them form pictures of this scene in their heads. As students identify details that help them form mental pictures, invite volunteers to highlight those details by dragging a finger over the desired words.
4. Click on the right arrow and read the Try It! prompt. Explain that students are to think of an anecdote they could use to begin an essay on making a piñata. If students need scaffolding, ask: *Where and when do people normally use piñatas? Who can help me create a mini-story about that setting?* Students may come up with something like the following:

> Piñatas are a favorite part of every birthday party. Grown-ups hang a colorful papier-mâché container from a tree limb or doorway. Excited party guests know that inside that container is a collection of tiny toys and sweet treats. They take turns swinging a baseball bat at the shape, hoping to smash it open. When the piñata finally breaks, everyone has fun collecting the tiny prizes.
>
> Did you know that making a piñata can be almost as much fun as smashing one open? Follow these steps to . . .

5. Guide students to understand that to work as an introduction, an anecdote must be short—no more than four or five sentences. It must be obvious how the mini-story relates to the topic of the report or essay.
6. Remind students to experiment with anecdote leads in their own reports and essays.

If you're using the SMART Board with younger students, move the toolbar to the bottom of the screen so they can more conveniently reach the highlighter and other tools. Just click on the vertical up-and-down arrow that appears at the end of the toolbar.

## Make Your Point

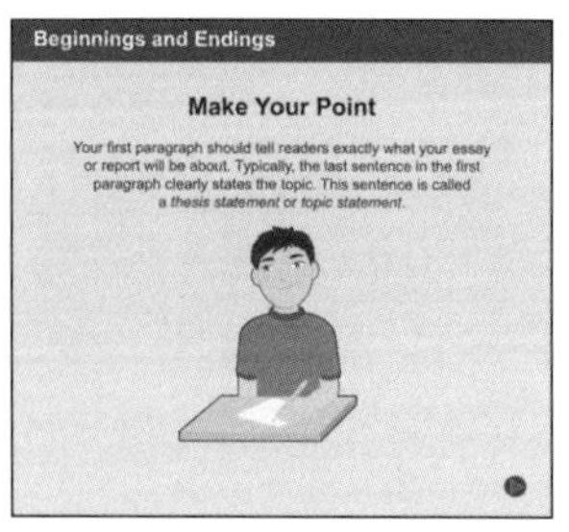


1. By now, your students should have a strong grasp of why and how to grab readers' attention at the beginning of an essay or report. Ask: *Once you have the readers' attention, what do you want to say next?* Explain that the next step is to give a clear statement of the main idea or topic statement for the report. This statement is usually the last sentence of the first paragraph. It tells the reader what the whole report will be about.
2. Display *Make Your Point* on the SMART Board and read the introduction together. Click on the right arrow to go to the next page, and then read the directions on the pull-out tab. Access the highlighter by touching the Pen tool and selecting the highlighter color of your choice.
3. Read aloud the paragraph about bones and then ask: *Which sentence tells us what the whole report will be about?* Elicit student responses, and discuss why the last sentence *(You should protect your bones. . . .)* is correct. The rest of the report will talk about protecting your bones.
4. Point out to students that this thesis statement uses a technique called *previewing*. It doesn't just tell us that the report will be about protecting bones; it tells us that the report will talk about two specific ways of protecting bones—getting enough calcium and staying physically active. Let students know that previewing is a great way to keep their essays and reports focused and organized. It is like giving readers a road map to the text!
5. Click on the right arrow and repeat step 3 for the paragraph about Old Faithful. Here, the thesis statement is "Old Faithful is a scientific wonder that never fails to draw crowds." Guide students to notice that this thesis statement is less specific than the first one. Can they still predict what kinds of details the report will include? Note that the report will probably discuss what makes Old Faithful a scientific wonder and how many people go to see it.
6. Remind students to include clear thesis statements (with or without previewing, according to your preference) in their own pieces of expository writing.

**TECH TIP**

Remember that all digital ink, including pen and highlighter marks, can be erased easily with your SMART eraser. Select the eraser tool, then choose the width that will work best.

## Full Circle Endings

1. Display *Full Circle Endings* on the SMART Board and read the introduction together. Have students recall the characteristics of a good ending that they observed at the beginning of this unit.
2. Click on the right arrow and pull out and read the directions. Read aloud the essay on planting apple trees. Point out that the essay is missing its ending. Click on the right arrow and direct students' attention to the prompts on the page. Challenge students to use the prompts to brainstorm some effective ways to end the essay. If you want, click on the left arrow to return to the essay. Remind students to look at the beginning paragraph and revisit some of the important ideas there.
3. Have a student volunteer move aside the apple to see one way to wrap up this essay. Discuss how the sample conclusion does the following important things:

- Reminds readers that there were six easy steps.
- Reminds readers of the purpose or main idea of the essay (how to plant an apple tree).
- Circles back to the ideas of "crunching" and "America's favorite fruit" from the beginning paragraph.

4. Remind students to follow this model and summarize important ideas when they write their own expository endings.

Beginnings and Endings

Full Circle Endings

As you conclude your writing, circle back to your beginning. Remind readers of your most important ideas.

# EXTENDED LEARNING

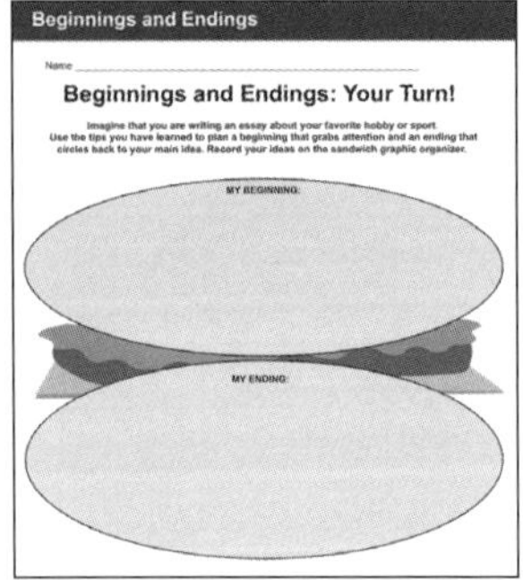

Beginnings and Endings

Name __________

Beginnings and Endings: Your Turn!

Imagine that you are writing an essay about your favorite hobby or sport. Use the tips you have learned to plan a beginning that grabs attention and an ending that circles back to your main idea. Record your ideas on the sandwich graphic organizer.

MY BEGINNING:

MY ENDING:

## Beginnings and Endings: Your Turn!

1. Print and make copies of *Beginnings and Endings: Your Turn!* Display the Notebook page on the SMART Board and distribute copies of the worksheet. Explain that students will complete this page on their own, either in class or for homework, to apply what they have learned about expository beginnings and endings. The page calls for students to write about a favorite hobby or sport. However, if students have already begun researching and writing their own reports or essays on other topics, this page is an ideal tool for planning the opening and closing.
2. Review the directions, reminding students to:

    - Plan a lead that grabs attention with a fact, question, wordplay, or anecdote.
    - Follow the lead with a clear thesis statement that tells the main idea of the report.
    - Plan a closing paragraph that circles back to important ideas from the beginning.

3. Once students have completed the activity, have partners share their work and provide feedback to one another.

# Meaty Middles

## UNIT 4

**In this series of Notebook pages, students will learn how to fill their reports and essays with perfectly constructed paragraphs presented in an order that makes sense.**

### OBJECTIVES

Students will be able to:

- ✓ Use an idea web or outline to plan out the body of a report or essay.
- ✓ Recognize and use main ideas and supporting details.
- ✓ Understand that expository writing is based on fact rather than opinion.
- ✓ Sequence expository ideas in an order that makes sense.
- ✓ Use transition words to connect ideas in expository text.

### TIME

About 3–4 class periods for Unit 4 (allow 15–20 minutes per lesson)

### MEETING THE STANDARDS

This lesson correlates with the following writing standards for grades 3 through 6:

- Apply a variety of prewriting strategies in order to generate and structure ideas.
- Organize expository material into paragraphs.
- Use a topic sentence and develop it with examples and details.
- Recognize the elements common to expository text, including main ideas and details.

### GETTING READY

Before students arrive, have your SMART Board ready to go. Load the SMART Expository Writing CD onto your host computer and copy the **4 Meaty Middles** Notebook file onto your hard drive. Open the local file. The first interactive page, the *Meaty Middles* menu, will appear on your SMART Board. To display the Notebook pages for each of the eight lessons in this unit, click on the button next to the name of the lesson.

# INTRODUCING THE CONCEPT

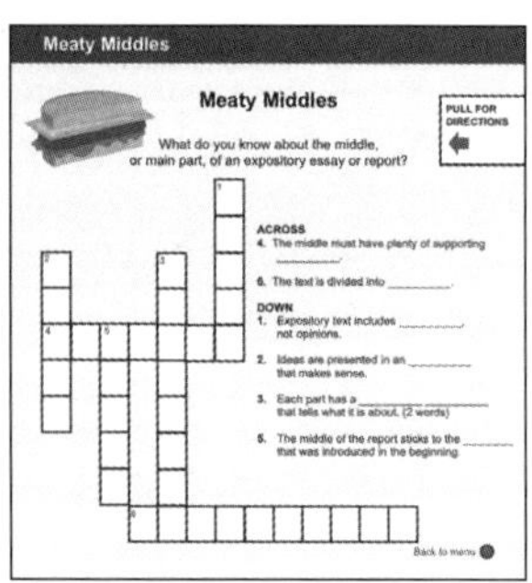


## Meaty Middles

1. Display *Meaty Middles* on the SMART Board and read the directions on the pull-out tab. Explain that in this activity, students will apply what they already know about the body of an expository essay or report to complete a crossword puzzle.
2. Read the first Across clue aloud. Ask a student volunteer to write the answer in the grid using one of the SMART pens. Repeat with the remaining clues. If students do not know an answer, leave it blank until you have answered clues whose answers intersect. Revisit the challenging clue, using the positions of known letters as extra support.
3. Explain that in the rest of this unit, students will explore concepts from the crossword puzzle in greater detail. These concepts include: main ideas, supporting details, facts (versus opinions), sticking to a topic, and putting ideas in order.

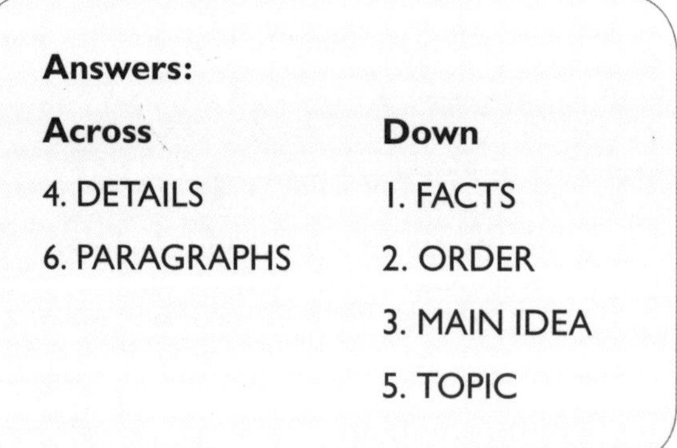

**Answers:**

| **Across** | **Down** |
|---|---|
| 4. DETAILS | 1. FACTS |
| 6. PARAGRAPHS | 2. ORDER |
| | 3. MAIN IDEA |
| | 5. TOPIC |

## TECH TIP

If students' pen strokes are not showing up in the right spots, it may be a sign that your SMART Board needs to be reoriented. Orienting ensures that your board is properly aligned and that finger taps, pen strokes, and other tasks will show up exactly where you want them. It is especially important to reorient frequently if you use a portable SMART Board. To orient, look on the startup menu of your Notebook software. The process takes about ten seconds.

## Organize It! (Part 1)

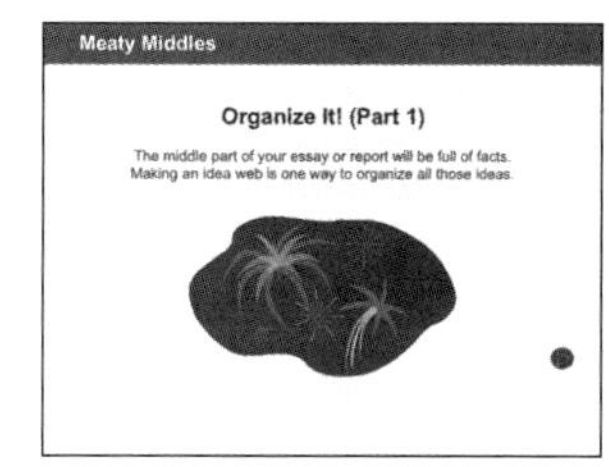


1. Display *Organize It! (Part 1)* on the SMART Board and read the introduction together. Remind students that by the time they start writing a report or essay, they will have collected a great number of facts from books, Web sites, interviews, and other sources. Explain that an idea web like the one shown on the following page is an excellent way to organize those facts and create a plan for writing.
2. Click on the right arrow to display an idea web that has been filled out. Have students notice the writer's topic (Chinese New Year) and subtopics. Point out that if the writer used a research grid like the one introduced in Unit 2, he or she could simply use each research question from the grid as a subtopic.
3. Read the directions on the pull-out tab. Remind students that the tools they need (the star, smiley face, and check mark) are on the Creative Pen and Shapes tools. Demonstrate how to access the Creative Pen with a fingertip. Choose the star shape to begin. Have a student volunteer tap the screen with a fingertip to place a star next to the report's main topic (*Chinese New Year*).
4. Return to the Creative Pen menu and select the smiley face. Invite three students to tap the screen to mark the writer's subtopics (*when is it, how are years named, what are some traditions*).
5. Finally, go to the Shapes menu and select the check mark. Invite student volunteers to place a check mark next to each detail the writer has included.
6. Discuss how the idea web structure would help this writer take the next steps in writing. Ask: *What will this writer do next?* Guide students to understand that he or she could easily turn each subtopic question into a main idea for a paragraph, then support that main idea with details from the rectangle shapes.
7. Click on the right arrow and ask students to discuss the question posed by the Talk About It prompt.

### TECH TIP

If you are looking for a particular tool (such as the Creative Pen in this activity) but don't see it in your toolbar, just right-click inside your toolbar. A full menu of tools will appear on screen. Drag the missing tool to your toolbar, and touch Done.

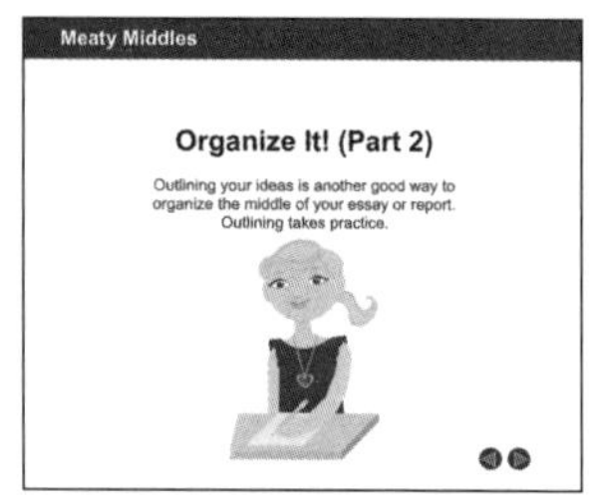


8. Next, click on the right arrow to display *Organize It! (Part 2)* on the SMART Board and explain to students that outlining is an alternative to webbing. Rather than using shapes connected by lines, outlines use headings introduced by numbers and letters.
9. Take a minute to point out some basics of the outline structure. Explain that Roman numerals (I, II) are used for big ideas, such as a thesis statement. Capital letters are used for subtopics or main ideas that fall under each big idea. Arabic numbers (1, 2, 3) are used to introduce details that support each subtopic. Point out that because an outline is for the writer's own planning, it is all right not to use full sentences.
10. Click on the right arrow and read the directions. Allow students time to read the incomplete outline and then draw their attention to the box of outline entries, pointing out that the entries are out of order. Demonstrate how to move an entry by dragging it with a fingertip. Then invite a student volunteer to read the first entry and place it where it belongs on the outline.
11. Repeat step 10 for the remaining entries until the outline is complete.

## What's the Big Idea?

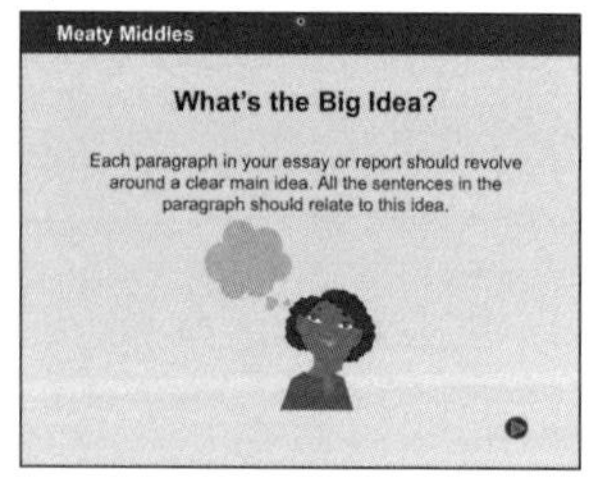


1. Display *What's the Big Idea?* on the SMART Board and read the introduction. Review with students the definition of *main idea*—the topic sentence that tells what the other sentences in the paragraph or section are all about. Remind students that the main idea is often (but not always) stated in the first sentence of a paragraph.
2. Click on the right arrow and pull out the tab to review the directions for the page. Have a student volunteer read aloud the first paragraph, then work as a class to identify the main idea. If you wish, have students mark what they think is the main idea with the highlighter pen. To check students' thinking, have a student move aside the clock image on the top right of the page. The main idea of paragraph 1 will be revealed: *Daylight Saving Time began in Germany during the first World War.*
3. Have another volunteer read the second paragraph. Again, discuss and mark the main idea of the paragraph. Drag aside the clock on the bottom right of the page to reveal the answer: *Two years later, the United States tried the idea.*
4. Point out to students that they may have read articles or books in which some of the main ideas were implied, or suggested, rather than directly stated. Explain that for now and for the purposes of school-related writing, students should always include a clear main idea for each paragraph.

## Details, Details

1. Display *Details, Details* on the SMART Board and read the introduction. Check that students understand the nature of details by asking them to name some details about your classroom or any topic you choose. Point out that details can include:

   - FACTS: Statements that can be proved true and tell more about a topic
   - DEFINITIONS: Meanings of important words
   - STATISTICS: Facts that include numerical or percentage data
   - EXAMPLES: Specific, real-life instances of the main idea

2. Click on the right arrow and pull on the tab to read the directions. Explain to the class that the page shows two cones and seven scoops of ice cream. Have a student read aloud the two main ideas written on the cones. Ask: *Could these two main ideas be part of the same report?* Guide students to understand that the two main ideas are part of the same broad topic (ice-cream cones) and would probably appear in the same report. However, each one has an original message and will call for different supporting details.
3. Have a student approach the SMART Board and read aloud one detail from an ice-cream scoop. Have the student drag the scoop to the appropriate main idea. Repeat with the other detail scoops. If a detail does not support either of the two main ideas, leave it in the center of the page.
4. Save your class's work and make a copy of the page for each student's writing folder.

## Just the Facts

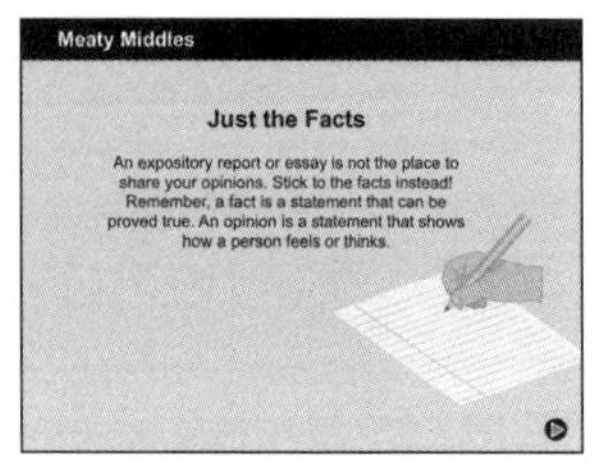


1. Display *Just the Facts* on the SMART Board and use the introduction to review the difference between a fact and an opinion. Emphasize that a fact is a statement that can be proved true. An opinion is a statement that reflects how someone thinks or feels about a topic. It cannot be proved true.
2. Click on the right arrow and read the page directions together. Have a student read aloud the first statement from the middle of the page. Discuss as a class whether the statement is a fact or an opinion, then have the student drag it to the appropriate side of the page. Repeat with the remaining five statements.
3. For each opinion statement, have students identify words that helped them identify that statement as an opinion. Examples of opinion signal words include judgmental verbs *(should, should not)* and adjectives *(scary, fun, best, worst)*. Talk about why these concepts are impossible to prove. Point out that what one person thinks is scary, another person might not think is scary at all.
4. For each factual statement, challenge students to think of a resource they might use to prove that fact true. Resources might include history books or Web sites, encyclopedias, newspapers, and photos. Some kinds of facts (i.e., Darla is 4 feet tall) can be physically proved by using measurement tools.
5. Reiterate that expository writing uses facts. Let students know that there is a genre of writing that uses opinions supported by facts and challenge them to name this kind of writing. *(Persuasive)*

### TECH TIP

Certain actions (such as changing pages while the Just the Facts Notebook page is still opening) may interfere with the animation and cause the statements to stop moving before they reach the middle of the page. If that happens, simply use a fingertip to slide each statement into the center.

## Order in the Report

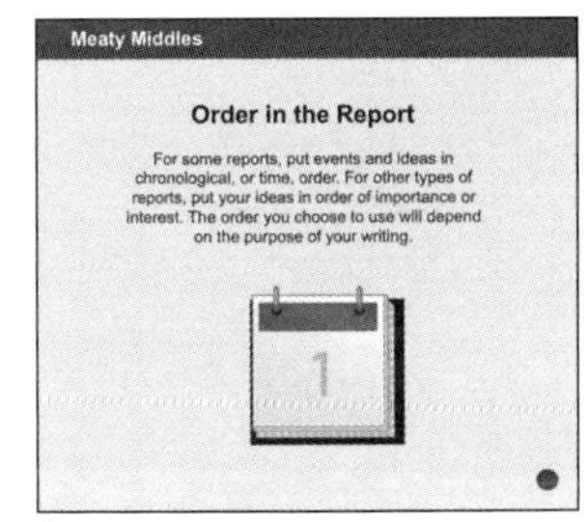


1. Display *Order in the Report* on the SMART Board and read the introduction. Explain that different forms of expository writing may be organized in different ways. To illustrate this point, ask students to recall what they learned about the organization of news stories in Unit 1. (All of the important facts appear near the beginning.) Let students know that two common ways for expository text to be organized are chronological order and order of importance. Which one the writer uses depends on his or her purpose for writing.
2. Click on the right arrow and review the directions on the pull-out tab. Remind students how to access the Creative Pen on the toolbar, and then read aloud the first report topic listed on the right side of the page. Ask: *If Kaylee is writing a biography of Benjamin Franklin, what kinds of details will she tell about? What kind of order would she put those details in?* Guide students to understand that for a biography or autobiography, chronological or time order usually makes the most sense. The writing might begin with the place and year of Franklin's birth and proceed to talk about his schooling, jobs, and accomplishments. Have a student choose a favorite style from the Creative Pen menu and draw a line connecting this report topic to the category Time Order.
3. Repeat step 2 for the remaining report topics on the page. For fun, allow each student volunteer to choose a different ink style from the Creative Pen menu (tie-dye, stripes, stars, etc.).
4. If time allows, invite students to name other report topics and decide which type of organization each one would use.

## Connect Ideas (Parts 1 and 2)

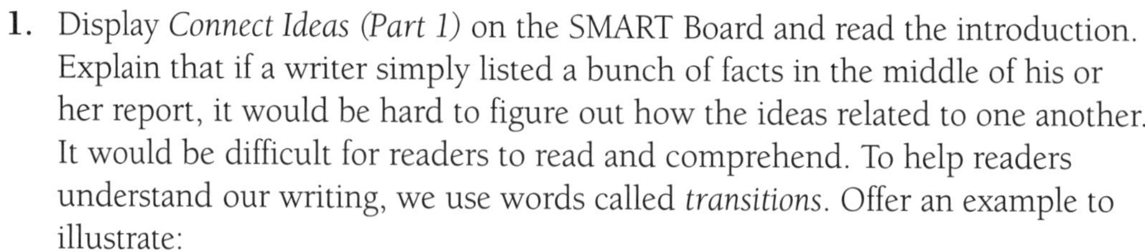

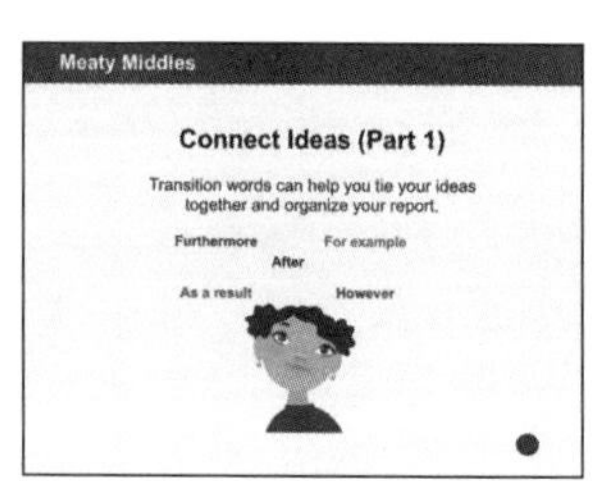


1. Display *Connect Ideas (Part 1)* on the SMART Board and read the introduction. Explain that if a writer simply listed a bunch of facts in the middle of his or her report, it would be hard to figure out how the ideas related to one another. It would be difficult for readers to read and comprehend. To help readers understand our writing, we use words called *transitions*. Offer an example to illustrate:

   - WITHOUT A TRANSITION: Kate does not have any pets. Her cousin James has three.
   - WITH A TRANSITION: Kate does not have any pets. But her cousin James has three.

   Point out that the word *but* prepares the reader to look for a compare-and-contrast structure. Without that keyword, it takes the reader an extra moment to make the comparison.

2. Click on the right arrow to go to the next page. Point out that the words in the box represent a few examples of transition words and phrases. Read the directions on the pull tab and explain that students will use the transition words from the box to connect ideas in the sample essay. Inform students that they will not use all of the words listed and they will use each word only once.

3. Begin reading the entire essay aloud, saying "blank" each time you come to a missing word. Then, return to the beginning and challenge students to find the transition word or phrase that makes the most sense in each blank. Invite a student to drag and drop the word or phrase onto the blank. Repeat until all the blanks have been filled in. Then go back and read the essay with the transition words in place.

4. Click on the right arrow to display *Connect Ideas (Part 2)* on the SMART Board. Point out that transition words fall into categories, depending on how they connect ideas. As an example, remind students that the word *but* was used to signal compare and contrast.

5. Read the directions and begin adding transition words and phrases to the page. You may start by adding the words from the top box in Part 1. Have students brainstorm other words and phrases as well.

6. Save and make copies of this page for students to keep in their writing folders. Encourage them to add transition words and phrases to the categories as they encounter them in their reading.

**TECH TIP**

When using the SMART pens to add text to a page, try out the handwriting-recognition feature of your SMART Board. Simply click on the handwritten word(s) and go to the arrow in the upper right-hand corner for a pull-down menu. Select "Recognize as (correct word)." To boost accuracy, make sure handwritten letters are not too far apart.

### Meaty Middles: Your Turn!

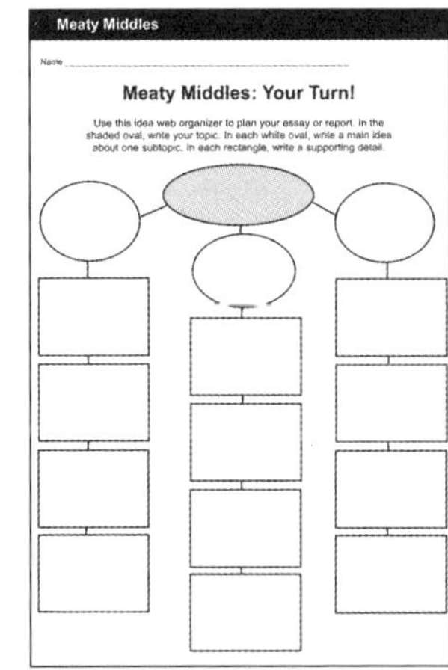


1. Print and make copies of *Meaty Middles: Your Turn!* Display the Notebook page on the SMART Board and distribute copies of the worksheet. Explain that students will complete this page on their own, either in class or for homework, to apply what they have learned about planning the middle of a report or essay.
2. Review the directions with students, explaining that they will record their topic in the large shaded oval. They will use the white ovals for subtopics and the rectangles for details.
3. To make the most of the activity, have students use a topic they have already chosen and researched for an actual report. If your students are not currently writing their own reports or essays, then assign a category from which students can draw topics (for example, states or endangered animals). Allow extra time for students to do research.

UNIT 5

# The Traits of Good Writing

**It's time to help students polish and perfect their reports! These Notebook pages will help students revise for ideas, sentence fluency, word choice, organization, voice, and conventions.**

## OBJECTIVES

Students will be able to:

✓ Define the writing traits of ideas, sentence fluency, word choice, organization, voice, and conventions.

✓ Apply the traits of good writing to their own reports and essays.

## TIME

About 3–4 class periods for Unit 5 (allow 15–20 minutes per lesson)

## MEETING THE STANDARDS

This lesson correlates with the following writing standards for grades 3 through 6:

- Apply a variety of composing and revision techniques used in the writing process.
- Establish central ideas, organization, elaboration, and unity in relation to purpose and audience.
- Revise writing to improve supporting details and word choice by adding or substituting text.
- Follow the rules of grammar, usage, spelling, and punctuation in expository writing.
- Proofread and edit writing for standards language conventions using checklists and other resources.

## GETTING READY

Before students arrive, have your SMART Board ready to go. Load the SMART Expository Writing CD onto your host computer and copy the **5 The Traits of Good Writing** Notebook file onto your hard drive. Open the local file. The first interactive page, the *The Traits of Good Writing* menu, will appear on your SMART Board. To display the Notebook pages for each of the eight lessons in this unit, click on the button next to the name of the lesson.

## INTRODUCING THE CONCEPT

### The Traits of Good Writing

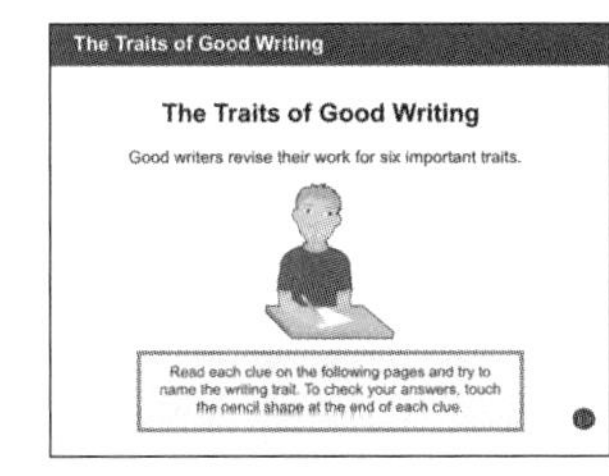


1. Display *The Traits of Good Writing* on the SMART Board and read the introduction and directions together.
2. Click on the right arrow to go to the next page. Have students read the first writing trait clue on the page and try to name the trait. Ask a volunteer to touch the animated pencil shape to make it move off the page, revealing the answer *(Ideas)*. Discuss this trait. Ask: *Why should a report have strong main ideas and interesting supporting details?* Discuss how these ideas form the substance of the essay.
3. Repeat the above steps with the second clue on the page. Again, click on the pencil shape to reveal the answer *(Organization)*. Ask: *What are some of the things we have already learned about the organization of a report or essay? How does a clear organization help your reader?* Review that students have already learned that a lead and a thesis statement should appear in the first paragraph, followed by paragraphs centered on main ideas, and then, finally, a closing paragraph that reiterates the thesis statement and matches the beginning. Point out that for readers, this sense of structure makes it easy to follow the essay.
4. Click on the right arrow and repeat these actions for the third writing trait described *(Word Choice)*. Ask: *What should you think about when you choose words for a piece of expository writing?* Answers will vary, but guide students to think about words that are specific, lively, and "just right." Remind them that some words (for example, *said*, *went*, and *very*) are overused.
5. Repeat for the fourth writing trait *(Sentence Fluency)*. Talk about some ways to vary sentences—starting with different words, making some long and some short, making some questions and exclamations. Guide students to understand that sentence variety keeps a piece of writing lively and interesting.
6. Click on the right arrow and repeat these actions for the fifth writing trait described here *(Voice)*. Ask: *What are some ways that a reader could tell that you care about your topic?* (Possible answers include: *I used a lot of interesting details and examples. I shared my enthusiasm for the topic in the lead to grab readers' attention.)*
7. Repeat for the sixth and final trait *(Conventions)*. Explain that this trait is sometimes called *mechanics*. Ask: *Why are spelling and grammar important in a report or essay? What might happen if you made a lot of errors?* Point out that obvious mistakes make it appear as if the writer did not take care to polish the essay. The reader may wonder how much attention the writer paid to other aspects of the essay, such as researching ideas.
8. Click on the right arrow and explain to students that in this unit, they will explore some specific ways to revise their essays for these six traits.

## INTERACTIVE LEARNING

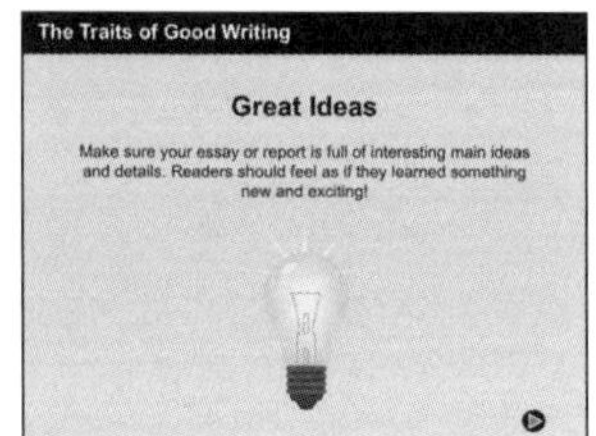


### Great Ideas

1. Display *Great Ideas* on the SMART Board and read the introduction together. Ask if students have ever seen a review of a movie or restaurant that included stars. Explain that in a review, stars are awarded for quality. Here, students will use the same technique! They will evaluate the ideas presented in the sample paragraph and give stars to the writer. If the ideas are unclear and need a lot of work, the students should award zero stars or one star. If the ideas are spectacular, lively, and engaging, students should award four stars.
2. Click on the right arrow and read the page directions on the pull-out tab together. Have a student volunteer read aloud the paragraph about Mauna Loa. Ask: *Do the ideas presented help you picture the volcano? Do you feel that you now know a lot about Mauna Loa?*
3. Survey the class to see how many stars they would award to the paragraph. Arrive at a consensus and ask a student volunteer to "clone" the gold star on the page as many times as needed. Because the star has been created using Notebook's Infinite Cloner feature, students can copy the image by simply touching it and dragging it.
4. If students did not award four stars, discuss some reasons why. Examples of student comments might include:

    - The ideas are OK, but I can't really picture Mauna Loa.
    - I don't know how tall "pretty tall" is.
    - How often is "sometimes?" Does it erupt every year? Every decade? This idea is unclear.
    - It isn't good enough to say it looks cool in pictures. The writer should include details that describe how the volcano looks.

5. Have a volunteer slide the text box to the side to see one way the writer could revise the paragraph for the trait of ideas. Ask: *How many stars would you give the revised version?*

## Sizzling Sentences

1. As you open *Sizzling Sentences* on the SMART Board, ask students why they think this page includes an illustration of an ear. Guide students to understand that sentence fluency is the trait that makes a piece of writing sound pleasing to the ear when you read it out loud. In fact, reading a text aloud is the best way to check for sentence fluency.

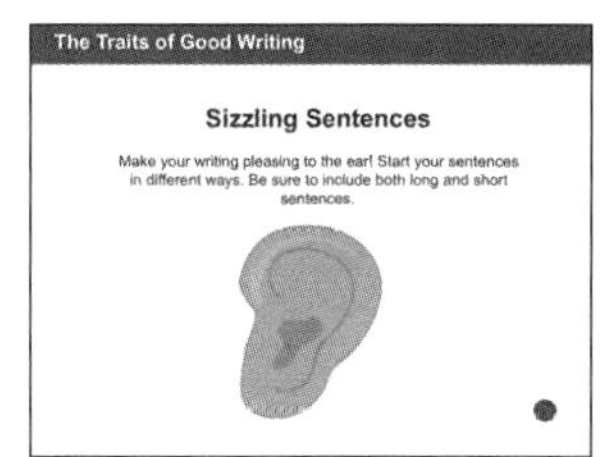


2. Read the introduction and then click on the right arrow to go to the next page. Read the directions at the top of the page, and then read aloud the sample paragraph about Harriet Tubman. You may need to read it more than once before students begin picking up on problems with sentence fluency. Use the SMART pens to circle and write marginal notes about any issues that students observe. They may notice, for example:

- Too many of the sentences start with *she*.
- All of the sentences are statements (no exclamations or questions).
- All of the sentences are about the same length.

3. To see one way to revise the paragraph so that the sentences flow more smoothly, move the ear picture aside. Read the revised paragraph aloud and ask students what they notice. Examples might include:

- The sentences start in different ways. (Some start with transitional words and phrases like *as a child* and *later.*)
- The sentences vary in length.
- The paragraph now begins with a question and includes an exclamatory sentence.

4. Remind students to apply these ideas for improving sentence fluency to their own writing.

Looking for space to record students' observations? In Notebook software, it's easy to create more room. Scroll to the bottom of the activity page and click Extend Page. Use the extra space to jot down your notes.

## Be Word Wise

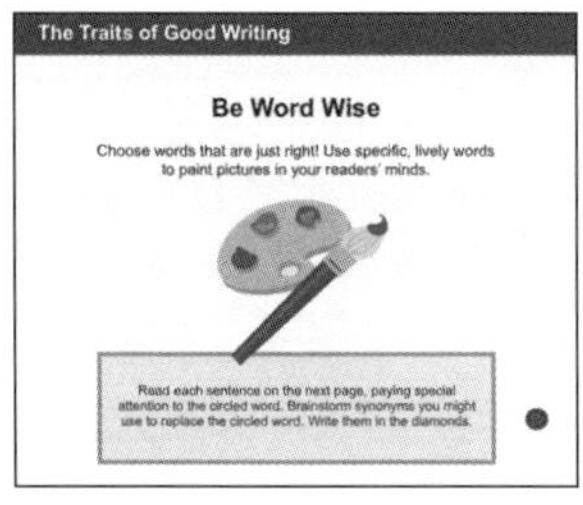


1. Display *Be Word Wise* on the SMART Board and read both the introduction and the directions. Click on the right arrow and explain that the circled words in this exercise are examples of tired, overused words. They are both vague, almost to the point of losing meaning. When we use them in our writing, we do not help readers make mental pictures.
2. If you wish, divide your class into two teams and turn this activity into a contest. Assign each team one of the overused words and allow the teams a few minutes to brainstorm more interesting synonyms. Emphasize that the replacement words should be more specific and livelier than the original, but should convey the same meaning (no turning *big* into *small* or *green*).
3. After a few minutes, have the teams take turns writing their alternative words in the graphic organizers. Award a pat on the back to the team that lists the most usable synonyms.
4. As a class, vote on a favorite word to replace the tired word in each sentence.
5. Remind students to pay attention to word choice as they write their own reports and essays.

**TECH TIP**

Is your writing not showing up on the screen? Try pushing a little harder with the SMART pen! You won't damage the SMART board by applying pressure with the pens.

## Stick to the Topic

1. In this activity, students will explore another important aspect of organization: avoiding extraneous details that might sidetrack the reader. Display *Stick to the Topic* on the SMART Board and read the introduction and page directions.
2. Click on the right arrow and read aloud the essay about the origin of the teddy bear. Challenge students to raise their hands when they hear a detail that just doesn't seem to belong. Pause after each paragraph to invite students to point out these details. As students point out irrelevant details, use the Creative Pen to cross out each one.
3. Check that students identified the following unnecessary details:

- They probably have puzzles, balls, and yo-yos, too.
- There have been 44 presidents so far.
- Black bears mostly eat berries, roots, and twigs.
- Cartoonists often draw pictures with a message.

4. After completing the exercise, reread the essay, leaving out the extraneous details. Discuss why unrelated details are a bad idea. *(They throw readers off track and distract from the main message.)*
5. Encourage students to stick to their topics and leave out irrelevant details when they tackle their own reports and essays.

## Share Your Voice!

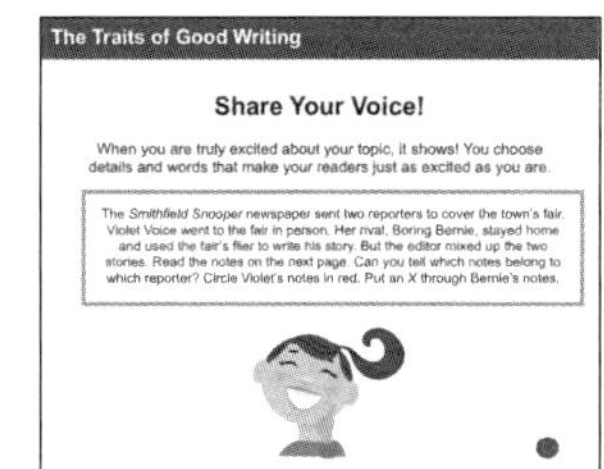


1. Explain that *voice* is a hard trait to define because it includes bits of the other traits. Writing with a strong voice allows the reader to recognize the writer's personality. The writer reveals himself or herself by sharing strong feelings, choosing words that someone else might not choose, and offering vivid examples and images.
2. Display *Share Your Voice!* on the SMART Board and read the introduction and directions. Discuss why a reporter who visited the fair in person would probably write with greater voice than someone who sat at home. *(The reporter who visited the fair would know interesting details that the other writer would not. If the reporter who visited the fair had a good time, that enthusiasm would shine through in the writing.)*
3. Click on the right arrow and point out that the reporters' notes appear in pairs. Both writers introduced the topic, both mentioned the roller coaster, both jotted notes about the ice cream and the pie-eating contest. But there is a world of difference between the two styles of writing.
4. Read aloud the first note about the fair. If students think it is full of voice, have them circle it with the red SMART pen. If students think the detail is a dud, have them cross it out with an *X* using the SMART pen.
5. Remind your students to use the trait of voice to add life to their expository writing whenever possible.

## Remember Conventions

1. Discuss how careless mistakes in spelling, grammar, and punctuation can undermine a writer's goal to inform or explain. Point out that such mistakes can make it difficult to decode or understand the writer's intended message. Mistakes can also make readers distrust the writer's ideas.
2. Display *Remember Conventions* on the SMART Board and read the introduction and directions. Click on the right arrow and direct students' attention to the Proofreading Marks box on the page. Explain that students will use the red SMART pen to make these marks when they find errors.
3. Read the essay one paragraph at a time. Pause after each paragraph so that student volunteers can approach the SMART Board and correct errors using the proofreading marks. (We found 10 mistakes.)
4. Save your class's work and make a copy for each student's writing folder. Encourage students to use these marks when they proofread their own reports and essays.

## The Traits of Good Writing: Your Turn!

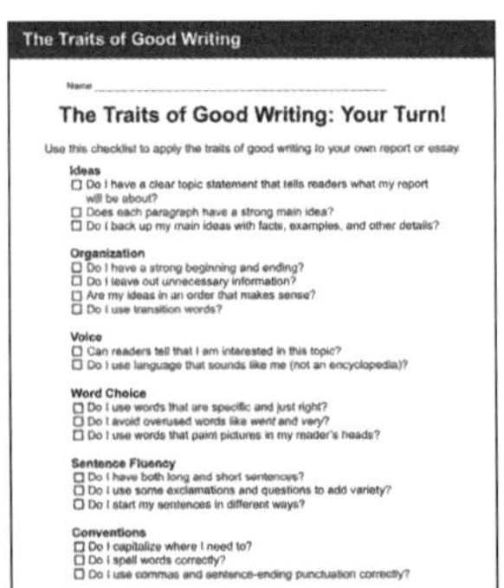

The Traits of Good Writing

Name ______________________

**The Traits of Good Writing: Your Turn!**

Use this checklist to apply the traits of good writing to your own report or essay

**Ideas**
- ☐ Do I have a clear topic statement that tells readers what my report will be about?
- ☐ Does each paragraph have a strong main idea?
- ☐ Do I back up my main ideas with facts, examples, and other details?

**Organization**
- ☐ Do I have a strong beginning and ending?
- ☐ Do I leave out unnecessary information?
- ☐ Are my ideas in an order that makes sense?
- ☐ Do I use transition words?

**Voice**
- ☐ Can readers tell that I am interested in this topic?
- ☐ Do I use language that sounds like me (not an encyclopedia)?

**Word Choice**
- ☐ Do I use words that are specific and just right?
- ☐ Do I avoid overused words like *went* and *very*?
- ☐ Do I use words that paint pictures in my reader's heads?

**Sentence Fluency**
- ☐ Do I have both long and short sentences?
- ☐ Do I use some exclamations and questions to add variety?
- ☐ Do I start my sentences in different ways?

**Conventions**
- ☐ Do I capitalize where I need to?
- ☐ Do I spell words correctly?
- ☐ Do I use commas and sentence-ending punctuation correctly?

1. Print and make copies of *The Traits of Good Writing: Your Turn!* Display the Notebook page on the SMART Board and distribute copies of the worksheet. Explain that students will use this checklist of writing traits to revise their own expository essays, either in class or for homework. Now is an ideal time for students to create polished versions of their reports or essays using a word-processing program.
2. Have students attach the completed checklist to their finished essays. Use the checklist yourself to evaluate and discuss students' pieces of expository writing.